For as long as I remember my life ha As a boy of four I would walk the short field and into the woods to listen and watch the bird life. I got to know wⁿ﹒ⁱⁿ they all nested and spent all my time in search of my feathered friends' nests, but back in the 1950's people were more orientated towards wildlife.

A rabbit was a welcome meal and most folks had eaten it. Fungi was another harvest and I only wish I had a pound for every wood blewit and field blewit I have picked throughout my life. The woods and fields were treated as an extension of your garden, to be harvested when the time was right, and not until. If a rabbit was taken out of season you were frowned upon, everything has a right to breed and rear their offspring.

I recall as an 11 year old taking a grass-snake to school and placing it on the Science Teacher's desk in a curled up spiral ball. Of course, Mr Vasey thought it was a rubber one until he came to pick it up and throw it into the waste paper basket. It stuck out it's forked tongue, he screamed "Oh, my God, it's alive" and ran off. I now know better, the snake would be left where it was to enjoy a peaceful existence to be observed at a distance. I was often given lines to write by the French Teacher for staring through the school windows at the fields beyond: Keeling 500 lines "Attention a la Classe".

At the age of eleven I wrote a poem "The Deer", though it wasn't that accurate. I call poetry a poor man's camera – memories on paper of life's events.

I owe a great deal to our countryside, I have harvested its beauties, collecting fruits, picking mushrooms, carving sticks, collecting leafmould and watching its changes throughout the seasons. It has also made me look at myself and how I, too, have changed. The one thing that hasn't changed however is that I still see the beauty now as I did as a boy of four, but with wider eyes and my respect for Mother Nature ever greater.

I hope you the Reader enjoy the journey through this volume as I have enjoyed the wildlife journey throughout my life.

John T Keeling

Spring 2009

INDEX

3.	Snowdrop		55.	The Journey
3.	Dying Elms		56.	When Thunder Broke
5.	Spring		59.	Bolt From The Blue (Hobby)
6.	Bert the Pleacher		60.	Call You Friend
7.	Free Man		60.	Cheetah
9.	By the Brook		61.	August
11.	Grebes		63.	The Jay
12.	England		64.	The Highwayman (Great Grey Shrike)
13.	A Way Around A Question		65.	Death At Dallowgill
13.	Jip The Lurcher		67.	The Falcon
15.	Magpie		68.	The Intruder
17.	Undertaker Of Space		69.	Not A Stoat
18.	Forty Horse Field		71.	Autumn Reaches Out
19.	Frogs		72.	Ageing Autumn
20.	Will		72.	Last Leaf Falls
21.	The Mighty Oak		73.	The Poacher
23.	Sounds Of Spring		75.	Hunter And Hunted
25.	Blue Flash		77.	Safety At The Sett
27.	Illusive Cuckoo		79.	Summers Last Days
27.	Cuckoo (chick in nest)		81.	Hare Aware
29.	March		82.	Do I Need You
31.	Hare		82.	November
32.	Thoughts		83.	Never A Child Again
33.	Through My Window		85.	Owl
35.	The Wren		87.	Mustelidae (Stoat)
37.	The Woodcock		89.	Winters Wealth
38.	Watch Water On A Boulder		91.	Monarch Of The Glenn
39.	Preference (Tramp)		93.	Black Shadow
41.	Watervole		95.	The Weasel
42.	I Will Return		96.	Home Return (The Lurcher)
43.	A Case For The Cormorant		96.	The Wildfowler
45.	Story Of The Hedgehog		97.	December
46.	The Skylark		99.	The White Hare
47.	Open Eyes		101.	The Tiger
49.	Orchids		102.	Snow
50.	From Boy To Man		103.	The Boxing Day Shoot
51.	Death In A Blind Hole		104.	Persistence
53.	Bluebells			

SNOWDROP

Little Snowdrop please appear
And tell us Winter's no longer here
Show your flower of milky white
Give the snow and frost a fright.

Stretch your stalk, head explode
Drive away the Winter cold
And when you do, my favourite flower
Then we've come through the darkest hour.

DYING ELMS

What can I say
Or what compare
Twigs and branches fully bare
Spring is here, others bloom
Yet deathly still
Hangs your head in gloom.

Beech buds burst
Like lime lit light
Yet there you are
No bud in sight.

Now Summer's here
Larks and finches calling shrill
Yet no response
Please tell me, are you ill.

Autumn returns
Time for resting, time for bed
But you my friend
No leaves to shed.

And Winter approach
All is drab and all are bare
Sad to say
This the only peace you'll share.

SPRING

First there's the Snowdrop
So warming and clean
The very beginning
Of a New Year's regime.

And out in the fields
Although there's the snow
But the hares do not care
Though its twenty below.

Also the rooks
With their raucous revolt
It's the first hint of Spring
That gives them the jolt.

Now faster and faster
It all gathers pace
And Black and White humbugs
Have joined in the race.

Excited and searching
But time marches on
For the frogs in the pond
Yet others have gone.

There on the muck heap
A snake joins the quest
With the sun on his back
He will be up for the test.

Out on a limb
A Thrush starts to sing
Hallowing all
To tell them its Spring.

BERT THE PLEACHER

A hard well weathered face
Grafting man you see
Boots and leathered lace
Countryman was he.

From morn 'til dusk would find
Bert working field and fen
A billhook he might grind
At the age of three score ten.

With faithful companion at his side
A trusty spaniel friend
His billhook cross the hedge would glide
And see the branches bend.

He'd lay a hedge so straight and true
No fault with eye could find
Whether skies be black or blue
Work was always on his mind.

FREE MAN

I love the land I walk on
Footpaths winding far
Away from people talking
See night times silver star.

Sunrise in the morning
Hue on new mown hay
The voice of young lambs bleating
Greeting another day.

So rivers ever flowing
And my mind a wild dream
Forever, always going
To places never seen.

For my life is in the country
On paths and tracks afar
Away from concrete cities
And fumes of motor car.

Always moving, never stopping
So relaxed and being free
Away from repetitious society
The only way for me.

So I keep on walking
Never finding home
Because all the world's your oyster
And all the world your home.

BY THE BROOK

If you've a minute or two to spare
Come with me to the brook
Rest yourself upon the bank
And into the calming waters look.

There beneath the alder's bowl
In reflecting heat of day
The chubb waits patiently
For food to drift his way.

And there, just there
The demoiselle lies in wait
Whilst on the reed across the way
"Azures" find time to mate.

But if your patience's strong
And avoid the urge to stare
A fisher on the root alight
That halcyonic bird.

A jewel of the brook
Make no mistake
A private bird is he
This reward so very great
An honour for us to see.

GREBES

Now droll winters days are done
Life steps up a pace
The grebes now put their blusher on
Makeup on their face.

Just to add a little spice
They both adorn a crown
To get themselves noticed
Whilst boogieing about the Town.

There are no better movers
Than these Great Crested Chicks
Strutting around the dance floor
Their Cha-cha-cha is pretty slick.

But when the discos done
Both require a rest
Its time to settle down
And build themselves a nest.

Just like all good parents
Offspring they think great
The mortgage's just been paid
Now time to find to mate.

So by and by the eggs are laid
Parents start to breed
A lady of acquine leisure
As husband brings her food.

Until coming home from work one day
His heart was filled with joy
There upon their Mother's back
A Girl and bouncing Boy.

She'd wrapped them both in Pyjamas
Her back they used as bed
Silver shimmering fishes
Is what their Father fed.

I find so hard to express
Life's moments that we've seen
Sharing time along the water's edge
With the disco King and Queen.

ENGLAND

England thou hast been
The heart of this place Earth
When I was young and green
I would be your serf.

To be born on your soil
So proud a lad was I
For you I'd sweat and toil
Fight for you and die.

But now you sadly lack
What makes others great
Can't we win it back
Or is it now too late.

Have all our brains
Taken heed and gone abroad
Are we still not sane
Or just we can't afford.

Have all our men
But turned to seed
England is but calling them
Will none of them take heed?

Or is it life's too easy
Just one long stroll
England we but tease thee
By picking up the dole.

(1976 My view of England)

12

A Way Around a Question

I ask a friend a question
But a smile is all I get
Did you hear the question?
No repeat it,
I forget.

Are you going to answer it?
Tell me, "Yes or No"
Then with a smile
Typical of her style
She replies then
"Shall we go?"

Jip the Lurcher

Rough of coat, long and lean
Not a stir of body seen
By the fire on the handmade rug
Jip the Lurcher, outstretched, his body taut
...And face so smug.

Ten o'clock strikes and the old boy wakes
A rattle of lead and the long dog shakes
Down the lane the Lurcher bounds
Across the fields to his hunting grounds.

Time went by on that moonlit night
As a passing cloud drifted out of sight
When all at once the quietness spoke
As the figure of Jip across the skyline broke.

Seventy strides the long dog was back
With a Hare in his muzzle, he'd still the knack
In the pocket, Sally bent
Homeward bound the mouchers went
Down the fields to the winding lane
One half a mile and asleep again.

MAGPIE

Vigilant soldier
Menacing glare
Sober and so wise
What victim is it at which you stare?
With those black beads you call eyes.

An hour has passed
Yet not you state
Apart from a gurgling chick
From razor shears, you says your beak
The quarry that you pick.

So hideously you bob up and down
On the pinnacle of your Throne
Gleaming purples, contrasting white
Defiantly defending home.

Then with final bow
And untold grace
Unharness like a Bren
Demolishing what you had in sight
An unsuspecting Wren.

UNDERTAKER OF SPACE

Caw-caw that insolent cry
That great black scourge
With its alien eye
Perched high in a domineering spot
Shouting the odds though querying a plot.

Caw-caw repeated again
That black butcher bird
Surveying his domain.

A sudden gust of wind
He takes to the sky
With the grace of a kite
Suspended on high.

Dead Rabbits, birds, all carrion he'd grace
With picking of eyes
Pecking of face.

Most birds of the wing feared this vulture of old
With dagger like bill and black mask so bold
But he too has God's chosen place
With black clad gown
Undertaker of space.

FORTY HORSE FIELD

All I ask
Leave it Green
Not a thought
What has been.

To watch the Corn
Turn to gold
As I have seen
And always told.

Skylark call
Shrill in ear
Plover dart
Like emerald spear.

Too late recall
A "D8" seen
To condemn
Or to redeem.

All the Earth
Has turned to black
Sultry, shaly, scaly slack.

Profitability, viability
They're aware
Conservation, nature
Do not care.

Deaf and Dreadful unconcerned breed
Pounds and pence
I call it greed
If truth be spoke
We do not need.

So.....
Please to me
Will you vow
So I may watch again
A grazing cow.

FROGS

We're not toads
We are but common frogs
You may find us on the internet
Or on water sodden logs.

But alas, no time to digress
Won't you come and join us
In our awfully sticky mess.

Grab yourself a partner
Strut your funky stuff
Do it under water
On the bank ain't good enough.

So come alive and take a dive
There is no second chance
Won't you come and join us
Welcome to the dance.

WILL

Will you be here
When the days draw in
To stroke my hair and
Soothe my chin.

Will you be here
When leaves have fell
Make my meals
And stories tell.

Will you be here
When spring appears
Run my bath
Share my tears.

Will you be here
When summers nigh
To say "I will"
Then so shall I.

The Mighty Oak

Of all the trees that stand so proud
The mighty Oak with its enveloped shroud
From the egg shaped acorn to the king of the wood
May be two centuries or three dependant where stood.

A great bulbous base of tumultuous size
From this part of its heart its life blood lies
Alligator style dun coloured bark
Equal to that of a Rhino's skin, would take a pick to mark.

Above that almost aorta type base
Several entwined main veins race
At the end of each, like that in man
A million and one capillaries run.

Though in man the cycle ends
But in the Oak to those leaves lend
As in the seasons leaves do vary
Spring lime, Summer olive, Autumn curly.

(1974)

Sounds of Spring

"Spink, Spink" the cry
The Chaffinch in the Chestnut tree
Whose once deaded branches now bud can see.

"Peewit" the call as the lapwing soars and dives
Over the newly drilled plough
He'd probably nest there when the grain showed through.

Bobbing and weaving down by the brook
A sound can be heard that is seldom mistook
So loud and so shrill
The sound of the Wren
Like that of a high speed drill.

A wood, a copse, a field maybe
The sound of a Rook
One might guarantee
Crowing and shouting
Way over head
As if saying
Winter has gone
Its spring now instead.

Blue Flash

Just strolling at the fall of dark
Wandering like I always do
When down the brook a distant mark
A dashing arrow of vivid blue.

I blinked my eyes as though to stare
But this happening had passed by
Transfixed I thought, How very rare-
What was it ,Where And why.

ILLUSIVE CUCKOO

I walked the woods
And foliage green
To seek a bird
So rarely seen.

To my delight
Within the hour
A Cuckoo called
From a sheltered tower.

I cast my eyes
All about this tree
But to my surprise
No Cuckoo see.

A minute passed
Perhaps two or three
The call it came
From a different tree.

CUCKOO (CHICK IN NEST)

I am a doctor Jekyl
In a borrowed nest I hide
Born with a malicious instinct
That only I survive.

Please do not take this personally
I am but one of four
But by the morning light
They will be found dead on the floor.

You might just think this gruesome
For there is no room for two son
I have to be a Jekyl
In order that I thrive.

MARCH

Now alas that Winter looses grip
Marches Daffodils air their trumpet blooms
The Thrushes song through notes so lightly trip
And daylight steals in mans once dark and dingy rooms.

The City lad looks through the glass
And quickly turns away
Transparent his thoughts of the great outdoors
On the computer starts to play.

Whilst by the dew ponds muddied rim
The Farmers boy's extended stare
Beckons friends to join him
For untold treasures he must share.

MARCH

The time is right and trust to chance
A thousand Frogs return to dance
None too early, none too late
For each and every Frog a mate.

Distracted by some distant eerie call
A joyous smile appears on the Farm Lad's face
The journeys end and the Curlews fall
Welcomed back, for home is such a special place.

Amongst the water meadows soggy bed
With searching toes and tilting head
Probes with sickle bill and attentive eye
Another Worm about to die.

"Where is Alice, do we care?"
Replied by the deeds
Of the Mad March Hare.

Fore whatever weather March may bring
He faces snow though almost Spring
Out in earnest to catch a mate
To do the deed and procreate.

And o'er the brow the Farm Lad strides
No place for Hares or ought to hide
With a mind to watch and eyes to see
The great outdoors.... reality.

Now time won't wait for he or I
Grip life the only one
Each and every month a prize
The year but Marches on.

HARE

On plough he'd play
Alert he'd always stay
Hint or thought of sound
Melts like ice into the ground
Though you know he's there
A clod of earth becomes the Hare.

THOUGHTS

I sometimes ponder on my thoughts
Whilst sat in my dog haired covered chair
Looking aimlessly into the sky
To the great wild world out there.

All those people
On this place called Earth
Breeding, feeding, sleeping, dying,
What purpose we have here
Deep I think
And deeper still
Wondering 'till my thoughts reappear.

Then I think
Has God with his powers cast
And placed us
Upon this expanse vast
Then I think
Yet again
Is God…Just a name.

Well if there isn't a God
Who made
The Earth, the Stars and Sun
By now I feel
Quite confused and tense
So I think of things
That make more sense.

THROUGH MY WINDOW

When I looked through my window when I was a child
Ash trees and sycamores stood proudly across the doc field
The impenetrable Blackthorn on the ragged slag wall
From where the Thrushes and Finches a morning would call.

A few yards in stood a gigantic beech
Whose spread-eagled branches towered above all the other
Trees reach
Only one footpath meandered through this haven for birds
And if caught walking it were in for stiff words.

When winter approached and all leaves had fell
Through the entangled branches a meadow could tell
Twenty eight acres in size I was told
And in spring till back end, cattle would hold.

Beyond the meadow though uneasy to see
Stood another large wood with a great rookery
Past this point was so clear again
The great open sky, which is always so plain.

THE WREN

"Listen!" there's that piercing shrill sound again
"What can it be?"
So clear and undulating like the morning rain
"Where is this creature that hides by the stream?"

He still calls so proud
Yet, still cannot be seen.

"Is it the tiny Pygmy shrew?"
With it's velvet coat
And eyes like drops of dew
"No!" it cannot be he
For the voice that I tell
Seems to appear from that overhanging tree.

"Hark!" there goes that contemptuous cry once more
"Look!" he's on the tree
"Now look!" on the floor
What a tiny fellow
Quite without alarm
Look at him with tail held high
Really quite a charm.

Three and a half inch from beak to tail
I doubt if very much more
But to hear his cry so shrill and high
You'd think he'd double that score.

Weaving in and out the branches he goes
Though looking for something
Which no one else knows
Then with intermittent flight
He casts his wings
And is out of sight.

The Woodcock

Secretive, secluded in some woodside verge
Or some dank and dismal bog
In ones or twos may converge
The barest patch you form your lodge.

And rare may I confess
Your call seldom recollect
Except amidst your Springtime flight
Your "Roding" calls I detect.

Camouflaged your dainty, frail form
So imperceivable for eyes upon to glance
Unless by some young to you just born
The movements of to catch a mere chance.

Your blacks, browns and buffs
Defend, by contrasting to your leafy plot
Until disturbed by the aimless jaunty boy
Your needle bill, through birches branches,
Thread and slot.

WATCH WATER ON BOULDER

Relaxed
Sound of running stream
Eyes unmoved, transfixed
So bright, reflecting, clean.

On boulder gushing waters part
Yet to engulf itself again
Cause an effervescing swirl
Of rapid flowing rain.

Then the wake gradually dies
And flows into an eddy
And now once raging water
Becomes so calm and steady.

PREFERENCE (TRAMP)

Haggard, weather-beaten, worn
Shoes in tatters, trousers torn
Trudging, trekking tracks and paths
Ignoring, not hating those that laugh.

Poking, picking, looking, lifting,
Survivor of the land
Minding, moving, walking, drifting,
No place he makes a stand.

Concealed, condemned, but not confined
Owner of no time
Dawdling, dozing,
For him no one to mind.

Peaceful, patient people
Your choice, you've made your stand
Loving, listening, liking
Living off the land.

WATERVOLE

When as a lad
If I'm not mistook
To recall the visions of the brook
Where upon the entrance to his hole
Sat the ever endearing vole.

But then as a boy as I progressed
The brook looked full of emptiness
My eyes would stare but he would not betray
The presence of his hide away.

Then from early teens into youth
Reality hit me and the truth
In England's green and pleasant land
Things where really not so grand.

Though betrayed by youth
I still have faith
A thing that can't be stole
For down that brook the other day
Came Ratty... Or should I say... a Vole.

I Will Return

I've lived in the country all my years
The place where I belong
So colourful, relaxing, quiet life
And to hear the Thrush in song.

Now a tear trickles down my cheek
For I leave my calm abode
To live in mans Rabbit warren
Of concrete and tarmac road.

The way we are today
Has decided against my choice
For money speaks not words
So I have got no voice.

But when the tables turn
And capital have reclaimed
I'll turn back those pages
And start the book again.

A CASE FOR THE CORMORANT

You are accused in the first degree
Of taking fishes from the sea
But to most we do accept
That with your bill you're quite adept
And whilst fishing along the shore
You're well within the common law.

However these deeds we may overlook
But to filch the Trout from the brook
Is but a crime, we would all agree
You are accused "what is your plea?"

When are fish are stole from pond or brook
There are those that's overlooked
I tell you sir far worse a felon
That upright most indignant Heron.

Twas the other day I sat upon along
And beneath along the bank came Nogg
In sombre mood he'd soon skewered
A Carp, which from the depths he'd lured.

Yes I fish, but the sea is bare
You human folk just won't share
No thoughts and no control
You tell me that I've stole
A Fisherman that won't repent
Me, a humble Cormorant
If I want to feed then I must fish
"Of course my friend, case dismissed."

STORY OF THE HEDGEHOG

Hedgehogs common, we used to say
Alas no more this statement make
On the step he'd find his milk
But nowadays the cats would take.

A friendly neighbour in the garden
Eating slugs and aphids there
If eggs were taken, we'd beg his pardon
Those were things he would not share.

But back again to that same old truth
That killer mans' been on the loose
As with the Osprey, Peregrine, dormouse and many more
The little Urchin lies thin upon the floor.

With DDT and Pesticides
Spread from the ground and from the skies
Little chance insects have of escape
And in turn, his toll does take.

If past these dangers he does make
And with his lucky life escape
There are still the dangers near and far
Of course the man, in the motor car.

The Skylark

Climbing, ever eternal spire
Minute by minute
Hour by hour
Ascending into the stratosphere
Uttering harmonious song
For all to hear
Like a referees whistle
So vibrant
So clear.

Into the blue sky
Dissappearing dot
Inconspicuous to eye
Impossible to spot.

Then without warning
Descends to the ground
To its nest in the grass
Yet not to be found.

OPEN EYES

Come walk with me with Summer scent
Breezing in the air
Where life abounds in sky and grounds
And magic everywhere.

Grasses blow to and fro
Butterflies are found
Beetles, bugs and crawling slugs
Are there to tell the story
Life's retreat beneath your feet
Lie there in all its glory
Duped with scent of days well spent
I bow to all before me.

May I address or just confess
The simplicity of life
When all appeals are the wonderous fields
And the gift of open eyes.

ORCHIDS

No Earthly man could hope to paint
In such sporadic sprays
Pinks, Purple and Lilac Whites
A thousand different ways.

But to each and every petal cast
As perfect as each other
Thwarted by your unique looks
Man the greedy Brother.

Diadems of beauty
Your warmth to me I grasp
For only days your blooms are rich
And know not long will last.

So let me treasure and inward take
This incidence in time
Through my eyes into my soul
And become a memory of mine.

FROM BOY TO MAN

From boy to man twas lifes plan
A young lad's only goal
You had a voice but little choice
To work down in the hole.

Always day and always dark
You had no sense of time
Just to do your eight hour stint
Down the ruddy mine.

You dug the coal there was no dole
The richest man I'd seen
For some men with pots of money
Have little self esteem.

Buried by the falling coal
This may well have been your shrine
For lesser man may have walked away
But those were good men in that mine.

And here today those same folk come
A case of déjà vu
A friend, a wife, a daughter
To love and honour you.

DEATH IN A BLIND HOLE

He'd escaped so far
His adversary far behind
Alas, he breathed relief again
An outlet he had found.

"Freedom!" he cried to himself
But to find himself entwined, cloaked
In Spider's web so strong
He struggled and writhed 'til he choked.

He did not want reminding
That death was at his door
And with new found leash for life
He struggled more and more.

Alas the bond he broke
Back beneath, into his earthy hollow
Menace close at hand
The killer he knew would follow.

Back legs kicking he fought in vain
To inflict a lethal scar
But terror was his assailant's game
And he knew no holds would bar.

He cried aloud to rid himself
Of this Ermine ghost of hell
Into a bind hole he jammed so tight
But his own trap had just fell.

Though he fought so brave a fight
Killing was the Fitches lust
And Conies squeal can hear now
Laying in that blind hole in the dust.

BLUEBELLS

In every month that passes by
I see a favourite theme
Pleasures that jog my mind
Whilst deep asleep I dream.

But often when at peace and rest
Or on a bank I lay
Images of wooded paths
Of bright blue glades of May.

Where butterflies flit and dance
Amongst the sea of Blue
An Inland ocean's pastel shades
Stretch far from field of view.

Canopies that cover
That keep prying eyes away
Where nature's secrets hidden
On the growing carpet play.

Tranquil, tasteful treasures
Reflecting shades of sky
Where one hour's purest pleasure
Takes but… a blink of an eye

And all around in harmony
To this sacrificial place
In honour to the Bluebell
Our woods again have graced.

THE JOURNEY

Few creatures follow me
I am the eyes of the wood
Very seldom seen
And so little understood.

Far back in time
Me and my brethren go
Long before the now common rabbit
And we're as wary as the crow.

Amongst the pungent ramsons roots
My scent disguised all day
Beguild by the beauty of the Bluebells
In man's crumbled ruins I sometime stay.

He's conquered most but will not conquer I
Look there can you seen that Wren
An unwise spot to build a nest
For I shall come again.

But this tiny bird
Really does me harm
With his buzzing warning call
He is the woods alarm.

Up there amongst the hollies crown
I see an evil eye
But if she lets me pass quietly
Then her young they will not die.

The waters of the stream I drank
But had left me full of pain
Where man has washed his hands
We must wait until the rain.

No not along that path
I fear that man may come
Tread quietly so silently
Along the rabbit run.

WHEN THUNDER BROKE

July the second
Nineteen Seventy Six
The sun beat down
Though permanently fixed.

Three months had gone
And still no rain
No good for the garden
No moisture to swell grain.

Cattle bellowing
They had nothing to eat
Parched grass by the hedges
And dust at their feet.

Cracks in the once water bound bed
Deliberately placed
Through which the water had led.

The sun beat down
With unmerciful law
Giver of life
Now taking for sure.

A few birds singing
Though in an uneasy tone
Swifts and Swallows racing
Happy to be home.

As though
By the snap of someone's fingers
You had been woken from a trance
The birds stopped calling
And midges stopped their dance.
Had the great one spoken
For all now seam't numb
Everywhere though in a prayer
Even the now hidden sun.

WHEN THUNDER BROKE

A faint rumble and repeated again
Like that in a tunnel
Of a far distant train
Gradually the rumble becomes more of a roar
The ground starts shaking
Have we started a war.

A thunderbolt crashes
Unknown out of sight
And like the Herons dagger bill
The lighting does strike.

Suddenly spots of rain
Are dotted on the floor
Disappearing as quietly as they came
And the ground
As though shouting for more.

Like a knife cast
Into a bag of grain
The heavens opened
And down came the rain.

A short spell of time
And the downpour did cease
The birds sang with replenished voice
And the sun appeared to tease.

BOLT FROM THE BLUE (HOBBY)

Last grasp of daylight
Sun slowly consumed
By the enigma of Night
Twittering in joyous mood
Swallows fast vivacious flight.

Ghosted by the golden glow
Harbinger of doom
Nothing did the Swallow know
A pillow feathered plume.

Single feather fell
Upon watching farmer's head
The day had rung its last Noel
Alone the Falcon fed.

CALL YOU FRIEND

I call you friend
Well, then I know you are
Nothing too much trouble
Nowhere too far.

May I take this opportunity
To thank you
For all that you have done
And one day in your hour of need
Your favour, I'll have won.

CHEETAH

Mighty hunter majestic stands
Surveys the grassy arid lands
Relentless stare, he must pursue
Victims of his uncanny view.

Gazelle has caught the hunters sight
His powers unleashed at the speed of light
Accelerates with unquestioned grace
No show of mercy with unrivalled pace.

A flurry of dust scathes the sky
Another innocent victim passes by.

AUGUST

So silent now the ripening fields
Who's nodding soldiers quietly wait
For the harvester and the grain to yield
Welcomed by an open gate.

Amongst the hedgerows protective shroud
Where Blackberry and Bryony make their home
Their vivid colours shout aloud
Who's searching fingers are free to roam.

And there a Chaffinches deserted nest
Yet back in May where fledglings spent
A time of growing and of rest
Now on the stubbles feed content.

Of how the seasons, so fast past by
And August nods, how time has gone
Just a Swallow in a cloudless sky
Summer now is almost done.

THE JAY

Aristocratic in our designer garb
Very little truth you portray
Mimicking all the other birds
In your ventriloquistic way.

Yet I cannot help admire
For your dazzlement inspire
Beauty, but a liar
On other Birds you prey.

Is it your ruse to confuse
Or merely an act
Prententious your intentions
But for beauty don't detract.

However I shall keep my distance
A Wren must surely know
Beauty is but skin deep
And you my friend, a Crow.

THE HIGHWAYMAN (GREAT GREY SHRIKE)

Conspicuous in your flash attire
On Hawthorns prickly pendants perch
With eyes of hawks and sickle bill
Through land and wooded grasslands search
For movement of some Mouse or Vole
That stray from limits of their hole
Though tempting fate...... And that they can
Earns no respect from the Highwayman.

DEATH AT DALLOWGILL

Two Derbyshire lads from towns had drove
For six score and more a mile
To a place on the North York moors
Where they'd rest and wait awhile.

But time was right the moon was down
Would give the men a thrill
To drop their nets and conies catch
There on Dallowgill.

Now Eric ran the long mesh off
And John he pegged it down
Around the wood down to the beck
All hollows had been found.

Laying low in the fields above
The rabbits ate their fill
Unaware two Derby men had set their nets
In the depths of Dallowgill.

Quitely as ghosts at night
The last net number four
The trap was set one more time
Like a thousand times before.

The winds were brisk and hands were shook
Night air began to chill
Black as coals on an unburnt fire
Round the hills of Dallowgill.

Upside of the gritstone wall they crept
The dragline in their hand
And shortly the drummers would fall
To the best man in the land.

In the Black of night you could hear the squeal
The rabbits paid the bill
With Musson......The best man in the game
And he'd come to Dallowgill.

From either ends of the nets they'd raced
To secure their hard earned prize
But amongst the longnets meshes
The body of Eric lies............

Tis there I lost my friend
To this day a great friend still
But he's dancing with the shushies
Eric's ghost of Dallowgill.

THE FALCON

High in the air he circles around
With large round eyes scanning the ground
His wing tips quiver in the open breeze
As he looks beneath him through the trees.

A thousand feet in the tussocks below
Little did a small Mouse know
That way above where clouds did ride
A falcon on the wind did glide.

Unaware the Moggy fed
Scurrying, hustling and bustling
Carrying food down to his shed.

One move too many
He'd been spotted
Alas the Falcon had Moggy dotted.

With wings fold in, down the Falcon bore
With streamline shape and razor claw.

Four seconds was all the Falcon took
As those menacing claws homeward struck
No sound nor movement did Moggy make
But to a tree did the Falcon take.

Head, ears, eyes as well
Five more minutes no Mouse could tell
Off the branch to soar once more
To hunt with wing, eye and claw.

THE INTRUDER

You may not see me
But I am there
Amongst the alder's knarled and twisted root
No man can spot me
But I can hear his thunderous foot.

I have no fear of dying
Amongst the ranting and raving of the stream
For havoc I have created
Destroying, waterfowl, vole and bream.

Maybe I deserve
This feeling that I've felt
Since man, he who imported me
And on a board he pinned my pelt.

But here I am, and here to stay
In a thousand waters lie
And on I'll keep destroying
Like the terns on the Isle of Skye.

But hush for now
For I hear a familiar sound
"Tally ho!" Tally ho!" – They've spotted me
Man… and his cursed Hound.

Not a Stoat

Eighteen inch nose to tail
Sixteen ounce, yet unfrail
Cream of coat smooth as silk
Eyes so cold as frozen milk.

Small pink nose and tiny feet
Yet he thrives on bloody meat
Heart so small and yet so big
Tackle anything, Mouse to Pig.

She lives to perhaps four or five
Yet needs to litter for her to thrive
Males called "Hob", female "Jill"
Quite a character, lots of will.

AUTUMN REACHES OUT

Now alas the summer gone
And autumn reaches out
To grasp remnants bequeathed to days
That seem so harsh throughout.

However in this declining mood
If you've a mind to care
And look at treasures left
For one and all to share.

Just because the swallows sit
And collect upon the wires
Do not hang up your coat
And rest beside the fire
Look along the hawthorn hedge
Early in the day
Bespangled jewelled treasures hang
Whilst their maker hides away.

Berries black, red and green
More precious than the stones Men bless
All along the hedges seen
This is life.....Not emptiness.

The flying tiger collects his fruit
And takes it to his lair
Whilst the last butterflies soak up the sun
For both they and I can share.

Beneath the chestnuts fading leaves
Where ripened Conkers fell
Merriment is had by boys
Only the fruits of youth can tell.

So when the sun is setting
At the ending of the day
Be rejoiceful like the Robin
Though Winter's on its way.

AGEING AUTUMN

Old aged one, when you where conceived
Do you recall the frosts in the morning
Those cold rotting leaves
Old aged one tell me the truth
Do you look back in anger and still wish you'd youth
Can you recall as far back as Spring
How vibrant, so young and how you could sing
Old aged one do you remember the time
When the days where so long and the sun always shined
There in your prime so handsome and strong
Why is Summer so short and Winter so long
Do you not fear old aged one
That this Autumn in life
And you'll soon be done.

No anger, nor envy of Winter or Spring
Not even of Summer or the beauty it brings
These we have shared…only look forward my son
When the last leaf has fallen
Then my work has done.

LAST LEAF FALLS

The limes through which my window peep
With melted yellow leaves asleep
For once again this year seen
Unveiled themselves of richest green.

Grey skies silhouette branches like a lifeless web
Months eroding like the sea tide ebb.

And now the winds and rains come down
Last leaf falls from its once golden gown
Bare as day when babe is born
Awaits the arrival of new spring morn.

THE POACHER

When rustic leaves have danced
Settled upon the damp and spongy ground
And racing winds speak through hairless copse
The moon's scythe shadows to be found.

Poacher travels like silent ghost
By moon and meadow and gibbet post
Crouching by the woodside hedge
Observing the silence in his head.

Even if one cackling crow may call
Twig might crack or stick might fall
Woud drift like Owl over hedge and dyke
To be consumed into black of night.

Menacing and cunning as the cat
With ears pierced like radar bat
For hours observe and then a gradual gait
Arriving at the Release Pen gate.

Would apply his toxic time served trait
By silenced gun and breech he'd bait
Pointing barrel towards the sky
Scythe of moon in line with eye
Silhouette sighted he starts his ploy
One by one to destroy.

HUNTER AND HUNTED

Just a wisp,

Tell tale air

Just a flicker,

Of an ear

Then a nose

To sight the scent

An eye

To catch the ear

A carpet

Red and green

If only... ... ...

No wind there'd been.

SAFETY AT THE SETT

Nothing passes my guarding eyes
Man, nor Mouse, nor Deer
Here upon the quarryside
I the Fox, have nought to fear.

The gravel path betrays
All those that may approach
Even the fury footed rabbit
Or humans that encroach.

In this excavated hole
Scents go swirling round
Nothing passes Toby's snout
Without them being found.

So it is here
Where our cubs are born
Another generation
For man to love or scorn.

Summer's Last Days

Resting on a Summers day
Green terrain and August hay
Relaxing, watching Swallows high
In so vast blue, cloudless sky.

Listening, thinking out loud
Waterhen with chicks strutting proud
Then I note a drifting leaf
And think of Summer's coming grief.

Soon Autumn will yet appear
Blue clouds soon disappear
Mighty trees look drab and bare
Smell of crisp October air.

No more Swallows haunt the sky
Another Summer's passed by.

Hare Aware

In meadows on September's Day
When Summer nights are waning fast
The Hares upon the pastures play
And feed upon the Fescue grass.

There puss feeds, ever on her guard
Those glistening eyes reflect
Selective in her choice of food
With long lobed ears erect.

Then with her twitching snout detects
That danger may prevail
Through athlete's legs project
Away, to tell the tale.

Do I Need You

Does Spider need the web it spun
Do Stars desert the sky
Does a Father love his only Son
Or Baby without its Mother cry.

Can Fish survive without the sea
Or Birds without the air
A Flower pollinate unaided by the Bee
A Fox breed less a lair.

Do not mighty Oaks need the Acorn
And the Ash as needs its key
All need something to adorn
And my something dear, is thee.

November

November dawned the other day
Fast and furious it spoke
With its fitful fist and iron grip
Stole the leaves, and branches broke.

To disguise its form
The sun brightly shone
Ruby berries on the hawthorn glistened
Now the leaves had gone.

Like pimples on a distant brow
A last grass feed for the grazing cow
Due shortly to retire
To warmth and hay in the farmer's byre.

As effective as the artist's brush
With consumate ease and little rush
The plough transforms the landscapes face
A patchwork in a special place.

The rooks and gulls there do alight
November serves and often yields
More pleasures that we first thought
In the eyes of those that love the fields.

NEVER A CHILD AGAIN

You, my little friend and companion of my lad
My pleasure most in life
I watch and feel glad.

Twas only three years ago
You too were yet unborn
Just happiness in mothers' eyes
Like a childs' on Christmas morn.

And now just look
At the infant age of three
You dress yourself, get a drink
Why, even get the tea.

Everyday I see you change
Like clouds up in the sky
Why don't you wait and let me watch you grow
For you grow so fast I cry.

Is it you cannot wait
To see what life's about?
Or the parent people
Who extrude the childness out?

Whatever it is with you
I closely watch till you are men
For older we must get
And never child again.

OWL

Daytime does he rarely stray
In darkened corners he'll hide away
'Til tell tale night does cast its shawl
And twit twoo that eerie call.

Then black shadow, down he'd swoop
On some unsuspecting night type group
Without sound nor winged beat
Death be dealt with lethal feet.

Night-time will he only prowl
So majestic, silent Owl.

MUSTELIDAE (STOAT)

Meticulous in your cruel art
Through Bush and Bank and Boulder dart
Wrything like the serpent and with ceaseless ease
Muttering to yourself, your prey you tease.

Intimidating Mustelidae canine chat
You warn your prey, the frightened rat
And dance about as though a game
Petrified to the spot the rat remains
And in decreasing circles you play your joke
'Till you lust for blood has him by the throat.

Only blood is what you taste
Bedraggled rat is ate in haste
A chic and mutter and of you'll go
To mock some other unlucky foe.

WINTER'S WEALTH

My wealth it lies on open plains
On damp and spongy moors
The solemn sun and winter's rain
And grassy verdant floors.

It lies up in the meadows
The Heron staunch and grey
In the bleat of a young lamb born
On a brazen winter's day.

The Blackbird and the Throstle
With their melodious morning news
And the Architect of the Oak leaf drey
From which inside he views.

And the sky of ever changing shade
A Kaleidoscope of thought
Never the colour of a minute passed
But a new dimension being sought.

Winter's Wealth

Of the ever rolling sea
And fetch and bring me tide
Of the ornaments its hidden
Still rolling, yet all before have died.

Mountain crags and crevices
From which the peregrine emits
The lordly calls from him to all
For others to keep their wits.

First primrose in the hedgerow's side
Frogspawn in the pool
And idle cows at milking time
Upon their cud they drool.

And the raucous in the tree tops
On their nests of stick and root
The squabbling rooks re-arrange their homes
Raiding one another's nests to suit.

The haunting scene on hawthorn hedge
Spiders dare deny
Grim consequences of November's grip
They're out to catch the fly.

Rolling hills, snow capped peaks
Where the tracks of hare abound
And of the sagacious rabbit
"Safely underground!"

And yet everywhere you cast your sight
Even in the winter cold
True treasures of life for our eyes to stare
And in our heart, behold.

MONARCH OF THE GLENN

Where Eagles fly
When valley sleeps
Smell of Autumn
Slowly creeps.

Hidden by Octobers cloak
Blasts a challenge
So remote.

Tingles down
The valley's spine
That age old act
Goes back in time.

Echoes of the Glenn retort
Apparition through the mist appears
Armoured with his sixteen spears
Come to answer those that doubt
The Monarch of the Glenn.

BLACK SHADOW

Black shadow of the night
What is it ails thee
Always dancing by the light
Please tell me how you see.

When at rest I've watched you close
With outsized ears and leather coat
Upturned in awkward pose
High pitch murmurs uttered from the throat.

All day on eaves you'll hang
'Til eerie fall of dark
Then when the belfry door does bang
Into the ghostly night, embark.

THE WEASEL

Orange Imp of the underworld
Your mismic movements fool my eyes
A golden Blur of where once you where
To melt beneath the briars.

To reappear on the dry stone wall
Once more I stole a glimpse
As your lithe and liquid frame
Poured through the Gritsones chinks.

Then upon the path, I had to laugh
From where had you evolved
A flippant spin that made me grin
Into the fading light dissolved.

Home Return (the lurcher)

Limping steadily wearily creep
Ancient armchair accepting her there
Covered in hairs from when she's asleep
Wet and tired, hasn't a care
Quietly laying on tatty old chair
Blinking and thinking then not a stare.

Whimpers..........................
Dreaming of running the Hare.

The Wildfowler

Dyke and drain, stubble crept
Hands and knees so bloody wet
Ten score yards in half an hour
Freezing limbs and belly sour.

All to squeeze that trigger small
To watch that distant greylag fall
But alas, this time in vain
For to the clouds the geeses' gain.

Smile on face he walks away
Consoled to know there's another day.

DECEMBER

A skeleton of the former months
All has been revealed
Nowhere to hide and little that appeals
You lack the lustre that once was worn
In those crazy days of May
Those scented fronds of the Hawthorn gone
And memories of yesterday.

In the distant past Swallows sang
How bare the wires...........
Not an upward glance,
Where once the Summer's fledglings danced.

Yet you have your moments and you show us so
You can call the birds to collect your ripened fruits
And tell them when to go.

That is when you provoke us with your power
The ravages of the wind
And gripping frosts up in the early hours.

But it is the benign snow
That lays the trap upon the weak
Then will not let them go.

Days of little light, you put us to the test
To feel December's worst,
You value Summer's best.

THE WHITE HARE

Away from Man's grasping hand
Where the lonely Eagle flies
Amongst the Heather and Tussock grass
Is where the White Hare lies.

In Winter's grip, tis there you sit
Alone and so remote
Bludgeoned by the driving snow
Protected with your warm fur coat.

Harsh and so severe
Yet reasons known to you
You choose this unforgiving landscape
With it's pristine and precious view.

You sit in sheltered silence
Listening to the mountains speak
Whose words are aptly understood
By those that live amongst their Peaks.

THE TIGER

Tiger tell us what to do
For all the worlds in love with you
I look inside the chasm of your eyes
But we all know, you don't tell lies.

We all know what path to take
To save the soul of thy namesake
And yet, for thy fervent power
Disgrace thee, and your parts devour.

Tiger, tiger, lithesome strength
An enemy of the human stench
When you've gone, what a shock
Another nail in the coffin clock.

Tiger, Tiger, Tiger be
All the things you mean to me
But blind are those that
Don't want to see.

Symbolistic in your pure trait
The space you need, and man can't wait
Can't we supply, the human race
A little time and precious space.

SNOW

Calmly it came
It did not mind on whom it fell
Greeted all of us the same
Yet we trees did not mind
Cold, but not wet, like the rain.

Never in the Summer do we see
But when in Winter's wrath
It comes to grip our every tree
And covers every path.

Pleasing after a dismal day
A pick me up
And may suggest
Spring is on its way.

Thoughtless o'ye refugee
You seek us out for all to see
And on our branches softly sit
From whence you came
you slowly slip

THE BOXING DAY SHOOT

Builders and blacksmiths and boys with their dogs
Estate workers and sherpers, men that cut logs
Diesel fitters and welders, accountants too
Solicitors and soldiers…women are few.

All come to pay homage on the Boxing Day shoot
Some wearing jeans others wearing tweed suits
Excited to be in our great countryside
A breath of fresh air and a dog at your side.

Whether a beater or shoot with a gun
Pleasures for all, young lads having fun
Fathers teaching their sons respect for the land
Old men smoking their pipes they just think it grand.

The tapping of sticks and echoing shot
The old telling stories that others forgot
Blue of the skies, a cock bird shows
A hare from the wood bolts off in the snows.

The village bobby dispensed with his bike
Talks with a poacher about things they both like
The past just forgotten for this special day
Tomorrow, if caught by the keeper he knows he will pay.

So here's to the Gentry keepers and Kings
Who keeps us supplied with these special things
A busman or fireman or barrister's name
For the love of the fields we're all of us same.

Till the end of my days I will always return
For this place in my mind and my heart will it yearn
For the everyday folk and the man in the street
Who come to pay homage on the Boxing Day meet.

PERSISTENCE

If you are to take a journey
That may take you most of life
Be prepared to suffer
Forward you must strive.

It is your mind you must satisfy
A goal of your own
Do not be discouraged
Then let your focus roam.

It is the taking part
Not just the getting there
Life must have a purpose
Both to look at and to share.

Though the prize may slip your grasp
All doubts you must resist
When to tired and weak to carry on
Then simply,just persist.